AF585067

Kind
JESS McGEACHIN

ALLEN&UNWIN
SYDNEY • MELBOURNE • AUCKLAND • LONDON

In this book you'll find
Many kinds of things
Some have slippery scales
Some have feathered wings

But kind is more than type
Kind is how to care
For creatures that you meet
And places that we share

Kind

FOREST MOTHER-OF-PEARL
CROWNED HAIRSTREAK
ZEBRA LONGWING
GARDEN TIGER MOTH
SAPHO LONGWING
GOLDEN EMPEROR MOTH
LONG-TAILED SKIPPER
QUEEN ALEXANDRA'S BIRDWING
OWL BUTTERFLY

Be kind to those who flutter
The giant and the small
Even things of beauty
Started with a crawl

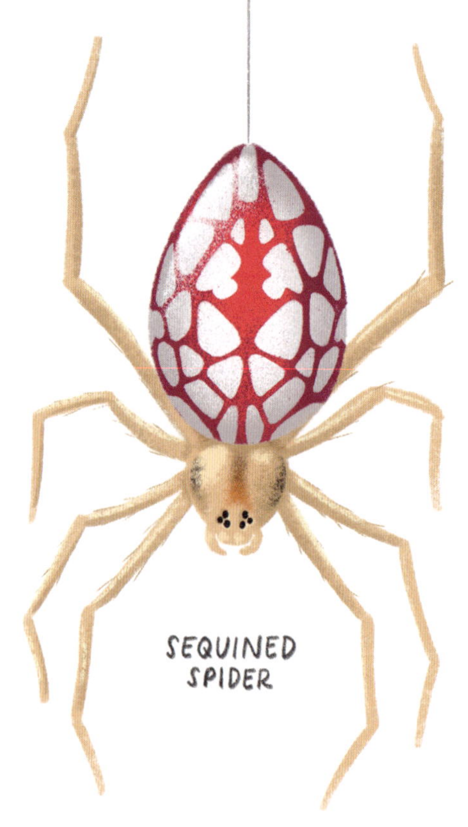

Be kind to those who weave
They knit and knot with ease
A home in silver silk
Dancing on the breeze

BUFFALO HORN SPIDER
WASP SPIDER
ARROW-SHAPED MICRATHENA
NORTHERN JEWELLED SPIDER
TRIANGULAR SPIDER
EIGHT-SPOTTED CRAB SPIDER
SPINY ORB-WEAVER
LADYBIRD SPIDER
SILVER ARGIOPE
BANANA SPIDER
ST ANDREW'S CROSS SPIDER
GREEN LYNX SPIDER

PURPLE SHORE CRAB
BLUE LAND CRAB
GOLDEN GHOST CRAB
SALLY LIGHTFOOT CRAB
SOLDIER CRAB
MALAGASY FRESHWATER CRAB
FIDDLER CRAB
HORNED
GHOST CRAB
PALAWAN PURPLE CRAB
ASCENSION
ISLAND CRAB
CHRISTMAS ISLAND
RED CRAB

Be kind to those with shells
It's where they like to hide
The hardest on the surface
Are softest deep inside

Be kind to those with fins
As they dart below the reef
A symphony of colours
Beyond the eyes' belief

FOUR STRIPE DAMSELFISH
PUFFERFISH
MOORISH IDOL
ROYAL GRAMMA
FIRE GOBY
RED LIONFISH
CARDINALFISH
BLUEHEAD WRASSE
YELLOW BOXFISH
CORAL GROUPER
LONGNOSE HAWKFISH
BLUE TANG
PAINTED FLUTEMOUTH
FLAME ANGELFISH
CLOWN TRIGGERFISH

BAIRD'S BEAKED WHALE

ORCA

HUMPBACK WHALE

BLUE WHALE

SPERM WHALE

Be kind to gentle giants
Who roam beneath the sea
Without their calls, silence falls
And so they must be free

BLAINVILLE'S BEAKED WHALE

RIGHT WHALE

MINKE WHALE

Be kind to those who waddle
In suits of black and white
There's comfort in a huddle
Throughout the winter's night

LITTLE PENGUIN
GENTOO PENGUIN
ADÉLIE PENGUIN
YELLOW-EYED PENGUIN
HUMBOLDT PENGUIN
CHINSTRAP PENGUIN
FIORDLAND PENGUIN
ROCKHOPPER PENGUIN
MAGELLANIC PENGUIN
KING PENGUIN
ROYAL PENGUIN
GALÁPAGOS PENGUIN
AFRICAN PENGUIN

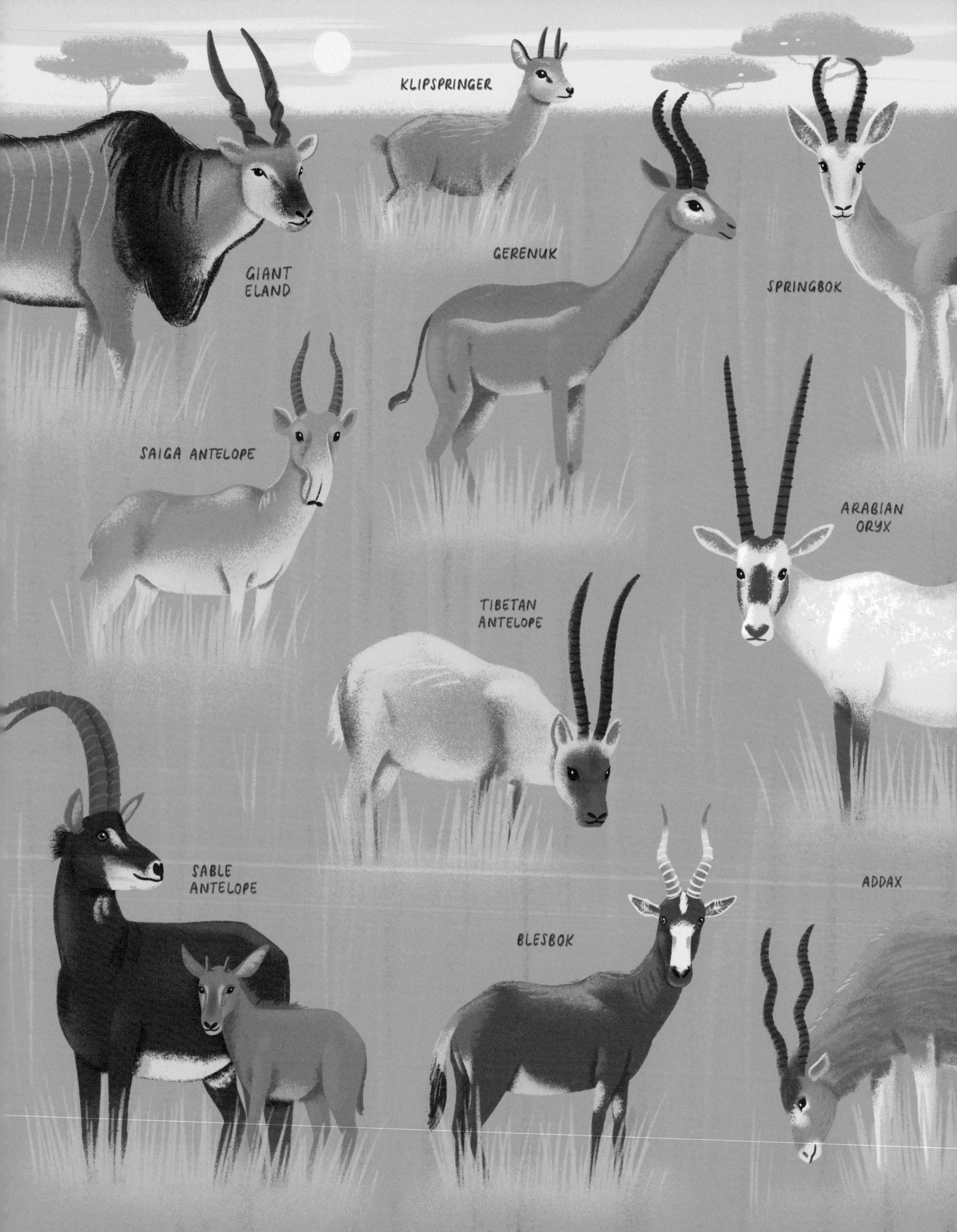
KLIPSPRINGER
GIANT
ELAND
GERENUK
SPRINGBOK
SAIGA ANTELOPE
ARABIAN
ORYX
TIBETAN
ANTELOPE
SABLE
ANTELOPE
ADDAX
BLESBOK

Be kind to those with horns
A handy thing to grow
For showing off to friends
Or taking on a foe

Be kind to those who croak
They share a secret tune
A choir in the marsh
Below the midnight moon

SHOVEL-HEADED
TREE FROG
SOUTHERN
CORROBOREE FROG
PANAMANIAN
GOLDEN FROG

BLACK-EARED
MANTELLA

DARWIN'S FROG

MARBLED REED FROG

DESERT RAIN FROG

GOLDEN POISON FROG
CLOWN
TREE FROG

POISON DART FROG

GABOON FOREST
TREE FROG

OAK TOAD

EUROPEAN GREEN TOAD

PURPLE HARLEQUIN TOAD

ARGENTINE HORNED FROG

WHITE-LIPPED PIT VIPER
EMERALD TREE BOA
MOJAVE RATTLESNAKE
MILK SNAKE
RED-HEADED KRAIT

Be kind to those who slither
For even though some bite
They'd rather stay asleep
Than wake up with a fright

Be kind to those who wake
While others start to yawn
A parliament is sitting
Before the break of dawn

SNOWY OWL
SPOTTED WOOD OWL
CLOUD-FOREST PYGMY OWL
EASTERN SCREECH-OWL
GREAT HORNED OWL
CRESTED OWL
GREAT GREY OWL
COLLARED SCOPS OWL
LONG-WHISKERED OWLET
ELF OWL
SPOT-BELLIED EAGLE-OWL
SPECTACLED OWL
LONG-EARED OWL
ORIENTAL BAY OWL
NORTHERN PYGMY-OWL

JEWEL SCARAB
FEATHER-HORNED BEETLE
BLUE LONGHORN BEETLE
HERCULES BEETLE
WEEVIL
BLUE FUNGUS BEETLE
TAILED NET-WINGED BEETLE
PROAGODERUS RANGIFER
HARLEQUIN BEETLE
FROG BEETLE
SCARLET LILY BEETLE
BATUS BARBICORNIS

Be kind to those who glitter
In gold and blue and green
There's treasure in the world
That sometimes goes unseen

Be kind to those with tails
Howling out their call
They might seem quite familiar
We're cousins after all

SQUIRREL MONKEY
WHITE-FACED SAKI
BROWN HOWLER
JAPANESE MACAQUE
GOLDEN LION TAMARIN
EMPEROR TAMARIN
ORANGUTAN
GIBBON
CAPUCHIN MONKEY
LION-TAILED MACAQUE

PLUTO
SATURN
NEPTUNE
JUPITER
URANUS

Be kind to where you live
This tiny spinning dot
The perfect place, in all of space
And only home we've got

We're nearly at the end
But not quite finished yet
There's someone left till last
That often we forget

Look at what's around
We're part of nature too
Be kind to other people …

And keep some kind for you.

A note about names

People like to name animals. Sometimes to describe what they look like, sometimes after the person who 'discovered' them or sometimes in fancypants Latin. This book mainly uses Western common names.

It's important to remember that many of these creatures have names in the languages of the First Peoples who shared the land with them, and before that they had no name at all.

First published by Allen & Unwin in 2022

The author would like to thank Sophie Splatt, Davina Bell, Caroline Foster and Alice Sutherland-Hawes.

Allen & Unwin
83 Alexander Street
Crows Nest NSW 2065
Australia
Phone: (61 2) 8425 0100
Email: info@allenandunwin.com
Web: www.allenandunwin.com

EU Authorised Representative: Easy Access Sys-tem Europe, Mustamäe tee 50, 10621 Tallinn, Estonia, gpsr.requests@easproject.com

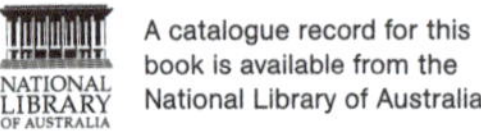

ISBN 978 1 76106 604 7

For teaching resources, explore www.allenandunwin.com/resources/for-teachers

Illustration technique: digital mixed medium
Cover and text design by Jess McGeachin
Set in 18pt Adobe Caslon Pro by Jess McGeachin

This book was printed in August 2025 in China by RR Donnelley.

5 7 9 10 8 6 4

www.jessmcgeachin.com